Wisconsin

BY ANN HEINRICHS

Content Adviser: Brett Barker Ph.D., Associate Professor, The University of Wisconsin, Madison, Wisconsin

Reading Adviser: Dr. Linda D. Labbo, Department of Reading Education, College of Education, The University of Georgia

COMPASS POINT BOOKS ✦ MINNEAPOLIS, MINNESOTA

Compass Point Books
3109 West 50th Street, #115
Minneapolis, MN 55410

Visit Compass Point Books on the Internet at *www.compasspointbooks.com*
or e-mail your request to *custserv@compasspointbooks.com*

On the cover: Visitors take rides on the Wisconsin River through the Dells in the amphibious vehicles called Wisconsin Ducks.

Photographs ©: Layne Kennedy/Corbis, cover, 1, 33, 39; Terry Donnelly/Tom Stack & Associates, 3, 6; Kent Foster/The Image Finders, 5; Craig Lovell, 8; Mark E. Gibson/The Image Finders, 9; Tom Till, 10, 12, 42; Robert McCaw, 11, 47; Hulton/Archive by Getty Images, 13, 22, 28, 46; Wisconsin Historical Society, 14; North Wind Picture Archives, 15; N. Carter/North Wind Picture Archives, 16, 41; Corbis, 18, 19; Scott Berner/Visuals Unlimited, 20; Patti McConville/The Image Finders, 23; James P. Rowan, 24, 34, 37, 38, 43 (top), 44 (top and middle left), 45; Richard Hamilton Smith /Corbis, 25; Jim Wark, 26; Mark E. Gibson/Corbis, 29; Courtesy of La Crosse Festivals, Inc., 30; Courtesy Eagle River Derby Track, 31, 48 (top); Reuters/Allen Fredrickson/Getty Images, 32; Michael Phillip Manheim/The Image Finders, 35; Kay Shaw, 40; Robesus, Inc, 43 (state flag); One Mile Up, Inc., 43 (state seal); Artville, 44 (bottom).

Editors: E. Russell Primm, Emily J. Dolbear, and Catherine Neitge
Photo Researcher: Svetlana Zhurkina
Photo Selector: Linda S. Koutris
Designer: The Design Lab
Cartographer: XNR Productions, Inc.

Library of Congress Cataloging-in-Publication Data
Heinrichs, Ann.
  Wisconsin / by Ann Heinrichs.
    p. cm.— (This land is your land)
  Includes bibliographical references and index.
  Contents: Welcome to Wisconsin!—Hills, valleys, and plains—A trip through time—Government by the people—Wisconsinites at work—Getting to know Wisconsinites—Let's explore Wisconsin!—Important dates—Glossary—Did you know?—At a glance—State symbols—Making cranberry muffins—State song—Famous Wisconsinites.
  ISBN 0-7565-0328-0
  1. Wisconsin—Juvenile literature. [1. Wisconsin.] I. Title. II. Series: Heinrichs, Ann. This land is your land.
  F581.3.H45 2003
  977.5—dc21   2002010107

Table of Contents

NOTE: In this book, words that are defined in the glossary are in **bold** *the first time they appear in the text.*

Welcome to Wisconsin!

Gunder Bondal arrived in Wisconsin in 1848. He and his wife, Kari, had come from Norway. They wrote a letter to relatives about their new home. "The land's riches and fertility," they said, are "impossible for us to describe."

Gunder and Kari worked hard and did well. They raised cattle, wheat, and hay, and they sold wood. Wisconsin is still a rich land. It has fertile soil, huge forests, and plenty of water.

Wisconsin is often called America's Dairyland. Thousands of cows graze across its rolling plains. Their milk is made into butter, cheese—and ice cream! Wisconsin is also a leader in making machines and paper.

Visitors love Wisconsin. They enjoy its pine forests, its sparkling rivers, and its sky-blue lakes. Among the deer and chipmunks, they feel close to nature. Now let's explore Wisconsin. You're sure to love it, too!

▲ Wisconsin is known for its beautiful countryside and rich farmland.

Lake Michigan forms Wisconsin's eastern border.

Wisconsin is shaped like a big mitten. The "thumb" is the Door Peninsula. It sticks out into Lake Michigan. Lake Michigan also forms Wisconsin's eastern border. Illinois lies south of Wisconsin. Minnesota and Iowa lie to the west, across the Mississippi and Saint Croix Rivers. On the north is Lake Superior. Michigan's Upper Peninsula joins northeast Wisconsin.

Huge glaciers, or ice sheets, once moved across Wisconsin. They scraped along, rounding off hills and filling valleys. Over time, the glaciers melted, leaving lakes, rivers, and wetlands. Wisconsin has thousands of lakes. Many of its rivers tumble down into waterfalls.

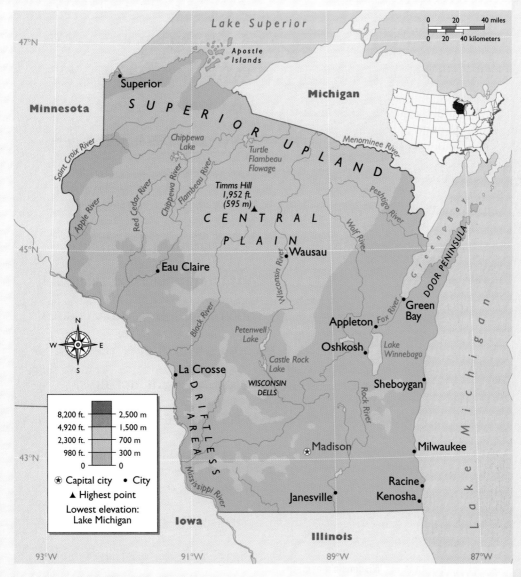

▲ **A topographic map of Wisconsin**

Most of northern Wisconsin is part of the Superior Upland. It ends at a high cliff near Lake Superior. North of that cliff, flat plains line the lake.

The Central Plain curves across Wisconsin's middle. It is shaped like a crescent moon—or a big smile! At the plain's southern end is an area known as the Wisconsin Dells. There the Wisconsin River has carved out a deep valley. Wisconsin's Chippewa people gave that river its name. *Wisconsin* is an Indian word meaning "gathering of the waters." In time, people called this whole region Wisconsin.

▲ **Visitors to the Wisconsin Dells can take a boat tour of the Wisconsin River.**

▲ Milwaukee is Wisconsin's biggest city.

Southeast Wisconsin is the Ridges and Lowlands region. The state's best farmland is found here. Steep cliffs and sandy beaches run along Lake Michigan. Milwaukee, Wisconsin's largest city, is on the lake. Madison, the state capital, is in south-central Wisconsin.

Green Bay separates Wisconsin's "thumb" from the "mitten." At the base of the bay is the city of Green Bay. Lake Winnebago lies between Green Bay and Milwaukee. It is Wisconsin's largest lake.

Southwest Wisconsin is called the Driftless Area. The glaciers never reached this region. It has high, rocky hills and deep valleys. The Mississippi River forms much of Wisconsin's western border. In some spots, rocky cliffs overlook the river.

▲ **Wisconsin's Driftless Area is also home to the state's largest natural arch.**

▲ **Many black bears inhabit Wisconsin's northern forests.**

Almost half of Wisconsin is covered with forests. They shelter deer, bears, chipmunks, and foxes. Beavers build their homes of wood across the rivers. Fur traders once hunted the beavers for their furs. Many fish swim in Wisconsin's rivers and lakes.

▲ Snow covers the top of a boulder in Devil's Lake State Park.

Summers in Wisconsin are warm. In the fall, the leaves turn bright yellow and orange. Wisconsin's winters are long and cold. Some people go ice fishing then. They fish through holes they cut in the ice. Snow falls all over the state. That's when skiers and snowmobilers have fun. When spring comes, colorful wildflowers cover the land.

Wisconsin's forests were once home to thousands of American Indians. In the 1600s, Menominee and Winnebago people lived in the east. The Menominee gathered wild rice, farmed, fished, and hunted. The Winnebago grew corn, beans, squash, and tobacco. The Chippewa, or Ojibwa, lived along Lake Superior. They moved as the seasons changed. Later, many other groups moved into Wisconsin. They included the Sauk, Kickapoo, and Potawatomi.

▲ **Blue Wings, a member of the Winnebago tribe**

13

▲ Jean Nicolet was greeted by Menominee people when he landed near Green Bay.

French explorers were the first Europeans in
Wisconsin. Jean Nicolet landed near Green Bay in 1634.
In 1658, French fur traders explored Lake Superior's shore.
Father René Ménard came to teach Christianity to the

Indians. He opened a mission near Ashland in 1660. The French lost Wisconsin to Great Britain in 1763. After the Revolutionary War (1775–1783), the United States took over.

Miners came to dig lead in southwest Wisconsin. New settlers were eager to farm in Wisconsin, too. Little by little, they pushed out the Indians. The Sauk chief Black Hawk tried to fight back. In the Black Hawk War of 1832, most of his warriors were killed.

Wisconsin Territory was created in 1836. In

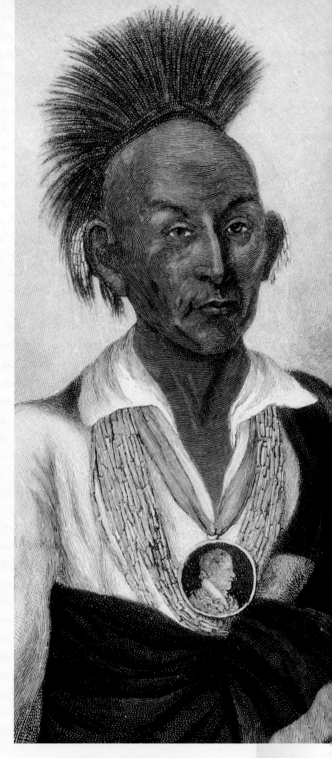

▲ **The Sauk chief Black Hawk**

1848, Wisconsin became the thirtieth U.S. state. By that time, many of the Indians who remained after the Black Hawk War had been forced off their land. More than three hundred thousand people lived in Wisconsin by 1850, but few of them were Native Americans. Most had come from eastern states. Others came from Great Britain, Germany, Norway, or Sweden. They grew wheat in Wisconsin's rich soil.

At that time, the United States was divided over slavery. The U.S. Congress passed the Kansas–Nebraska Act in 1854. This law said the people in new territories could choose to have slavery if they wished. This angered many Wisconsinites. They were against the spread of slavery. They met in Ripon and formed the Republican Party. Many powerful people joined the Republicans. One was Abraham Lincoln. He was elected president in 1860. He guided the country through the bloody Civil War (1861–1865).

Dairy farming was becoming a big business in Wisconsin in the mid-1800s. Farmers raised dairy

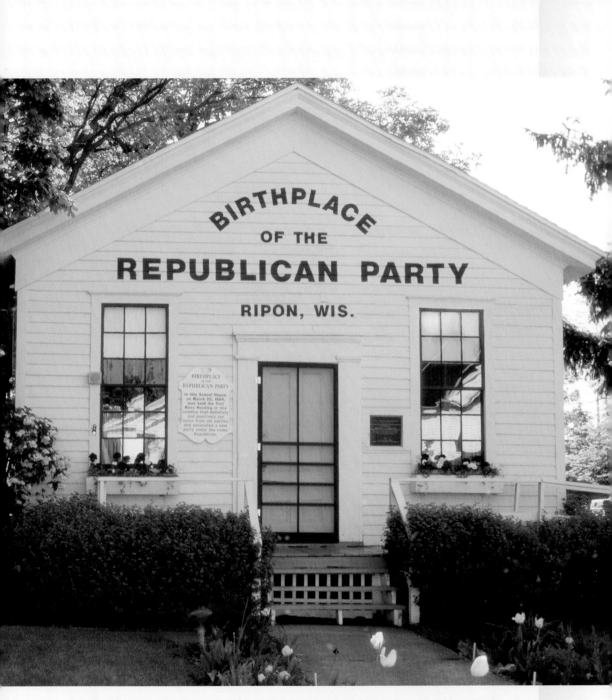

▲ Wisconsinites met in the Little White Schoolhouse in Ripon to form the Republican Party.

▲ By the early 1900s, logging had become a big business in Wisconsin.

cows for milk, cream, butter, and cheese. Meanwhile,

the lumber **industry** spread across northern Wisconsin.

Many Republican leaders were giving special favors to big companies. Robert La Follette Sr. opposed this kind of government. La Follette began Wisconsin's Progressive period when he became the state's governor in 1901. His many reforms made life easier for workers.

By the 1920s, Wisconsin led the nation in dairy products. Its factories were making paper and machines, too. In the 1950s, however, dairy farms began losing money. Americans were eating more low-fat foods. That meant sales of butter, cheese, and cream

▲ Robert La Follette Sr.

dropped. The state began to rely even more on manufacturing.

Today, Wisconsin is doing well. It sells its factory and farm products worldwide. Tourism is a big industry, as well. Visitors love Wisconsin's scenic beauty.

▲ **Wisconsin's legislature meets in the state capitol in Madison.**

Wisconsin's state government is much like the U.S. government. It has three branches—legislative, executive, and judicial. This is a smart way to run a government. The three branches keep a check on one another. They make sure no branch gets too powerful.

The legislative branch makes the state laws. It also decides how the state will spend its money. Voters elect their lawmakers to serve in Wisconsin's legislature. It has two houses, or parts. One is the thirty-three-member senate. The other is the ninety-nine-member assembly. They all meet in the state capitol in Madison.

The executive branch makes sure the state's laws are carried out. Wisconsin's governor is the head of the executive branch. Wisconsinites vote to choose a governor

▲ **A geopolitical map of Wisconsin**

every four years. The
governor can serve any
number of terms. Voters
also elect five other executive officers. In addition,
the governor appoints
people to hundreds of
other state jobs.

The judicial branch is
made up of judges. The
judges know all about
Wisconsin's laws. They
listen to cases in court.
Then they decide whether
a law has been broken.

▲ William Rehnquist

Judges in Wisconsin are elected by the voters. Wisconsin's
highest court is the state supreme court. Wisconsin's most
famous judge is William Rehnquist. He joined the U.S.
Supreme Court in 1972. In 1986, he became the court's
chief justice.

Wisconsin is divided into seventy-two counties. Voters in each county elect a board of supervisors. Cities, towns, and villages each have local governments. A mayor and city council govern most cities. Some cities elect a city manager rather than a mayor. Villages have a board of trustees, and towns have a board of supervisors. In some towns, voters get together at a town meeting. There they elect officers and take care of other business matters.

▲ County business is conducted in the Brown County Courthouse in Green Bay.

Wisconsinites at Work

When you say "cheese!"—think of Wisconsin. It makes more cheese than any other state. More than a million dairy cows graze across Wisconsin! Farmers also raise beef cattle, turkeys, chickens, and pigs. Corn is Wisconsin's major crop. Other important crops are soybeans, oats, wheat, and potatoes. In 2000, Wisconsin was the top state for snap beans. It ranked third in oats, sweet corn, and green peas. Wisconsinites also grow cranberries, cherries, and apples.

▲ **Much of the corn grown in Wisconsin is used to feed livestock.**

Machines are Wisconsin's leading factory products. Some examples are engines, cranes, heaters, and refrigerators. Some factories make food products, including cheese,

▲ In this Wisconsin factory, cheese is made in huge copper vats.

▲ A gravel pit near Madison

butter, ice cream, and beer. Other factories make metal goods such as knives and cans. Wisconsin also makes paper, cars, computers, and chemicals.

Sand, gravel, and crushed stone are Wisconsin's leading minerals. They are mainly used for making buildings and roads. Wisconsin ranks second in silica stone and third in dimension stone. Dimension stone, such as limestone and granite, can be removed in huge blocks.

All these things are products that Wisconsin sells. However, most Wisconsin workers sell services rather than products. They may work in schools, hospitals, banks, stores, or offices. Some serve tourists in recreation areas. They all use their skills to help others.

▲ Movie actor Spencer Tracy was born in Milwaukee.

Some of America's best-loved people are Wisconsinites. Fans of older movies love Orson Welles, Don Ameche, and Spencer Tracy. For younger folks, there's Gene Wilder and Chris Farley. Author Laura Ingalls Wilder wrote the popular Little House books. Georgia O'Keeffe made giant paintings of colorful flowers. Frank Lloyd Wright's buildings are found all over the world.

In 2000, there were 5,363,675 people in Wisconsin. That made it eighteenth in population among all the states. Milwaukee is the state's largest city. More than one of every four Wisconsinites lives in the Milwaukee area. The second-

▲ Agricultural Hall is on the University of Wisconsin's campus in Madison.

largest city is Madison, the state capital. The University of
Wisconsin's main campus is in Madison. Next in size are
Green Bay, Kenosha, and Racine. Southern Wisconsin is much
more heavily settled than the north.

More than half of all Wisconsinites have German roots.
Some have Irish, Polish, or English **ancestors.** Others came
from Scandinavian countries—Norway, Sweden, and

▲ **Many Wisconsin towns, including La Crosse, hold Oktoberfest celebrations.**

Denmark. About one of every twenty residents is African-American. Others belong to Asian or Native American **cultures.** The Chippewa and Menominee are the largest Indian groups.

Some Wisconsin festivals celebrate native cultures. In the fall, many towns hold traditional German festivals called Oktoberfests. They feature beer and German food and music. Stoughton holds an annual Syttende Mai festival to celebrate Norway's Independence Day. Oneida Indians hold a powwow in Oneida every July.

People come from miles around for Milwaukee's Summerfest in July. It's a huge lakefront music festival. July also brings Milwaukee's Great Circus Parade. It celebrates the fact that Wisconsin was once the home of many of the nation's leading circuses. Clowns, circus wagons, and caged animals parade through town. When winter comes, Wisconsin hosts winter sports races. One is the Birkebeiner, the nation's biggest cross-country ski race. Another is the World Championship Snowmobile Derby at Eagle River.

▲ Fans cheer for the snowmobile racers at Eagle River.

▲ The Green Bay Packers have won three of their four Super Bowl games.

Football season is an exciting time in Wisconsin. That's when the Green Bay Packers play. They've competed in four Super Bowls. Vince Lombardi was their famous coach in the 1960s. The Milwaukee Brewers are Wisconsin's major-league baseball team. They made it to the World Series in 1982. Wisconsin's basketball stars are the Milwaukee Bucks.

Let's Explore Wisconsin!

How did Wisconsin's **pioneers** live? See for yourself at Old World Wisconsin. You'll visit German, Polish, Norwegian, Danish, Finnish, and African-American farms. Chat with shoemakers, **blacksmiths,** and other workers. They're happy to show you how they work.

▲ At Old World Wisconsin, workers demonstrate nineteenth-century farming.

▲ **This building in Little Norway was modeled after a twelfth-century Norwegian church. It has dragon heads on the roof.**

That's just one of Wisconsin's many pioneer villages. Another is Little Norway in Blue Mounds. New Glarus has the Swiss Historical Village, and Heritage Hill is in Green Bay.

Want to stand in the mouth of a giant fish? Then visit the National Freshwater Fishing Hall of Fame. It's located in Hayward and is built like a giant muskie. Muskie is short for muskellunge, the state fish.

Would you like to control a robot? How about learning to move a mountain? Then visit Milwaukee's Discovery World. It has many exciting hands-on activities.

At Milwaukee Public Museum, you'll walk among free-flying butterflies. You'll also explore Asia, Africa, and the

▲ **The National Freshwater Fishing Hall of Fame in Hayward is hard to miss!**

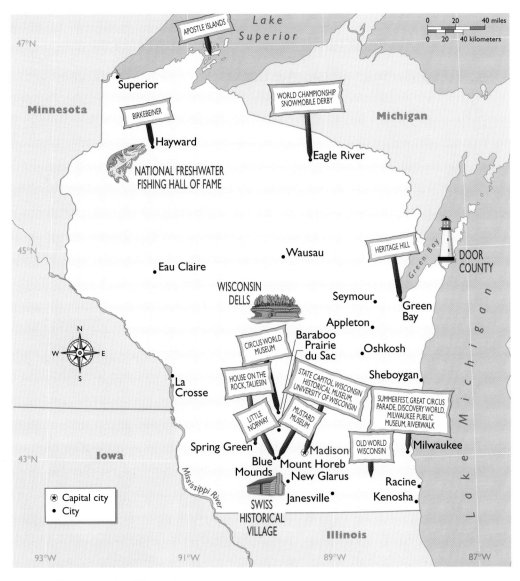

Lake Superior

47°N

APOSTLE ISLANDS

0 20 40 miles
0 20 40 kilometers

Minnesota

Superior

BIRKEBEINER

Hayward

NATIONAL FRESHWATER
FISHING HALL OF FAME

WORLD CHAMPIONSHIP
SNOWMOBILE DERBY

Eagle River

Michigan

45°N

Eau Claire

Wausau

WISCONSIN
DELLS

HERITAGE HILL

Green Bay

DOOR
COUNTY

Seymour

Green
Bay

Appleton

CIRCUS WORLD
MUSEUM

Baraboo
Prairie
du Sac

Oshkosh

Sheboygan

La
Crosse

HOUSE ON THE
ROCK, TALIESIN

STATE CAPITOL WISCONSIN
HISTORICAL MUSEUM,
UNIVERSITY OF WISCONSIN

SUMMERFEST, GREAT CIRCUS
PARADE, DISCOVERY WORLD,
MILWAUKEE PUBLIC
MUSEUM, RIVERWALK

LITTLE
NORWAY

MUSTARD
MUSEUM

43°N

Iowa

Spring Green

Blue
Mounds

Madison

OLD WORLD
WISCONSIN

Milwaukee

Mount Horeb

New Glarus

Mississippi River

Janesville

SWISS
HISTORICAL
VILLAGE

Racine

Kenosha

Lake Michigan

Illinois

Capital city
City

93°W

91°W

89°W

87°W

▲ Places to visit in Wisconsin

dinosaurs' world. This is one of three museums along
Milwaukee's Riverwalk. Huge mansions line the lakeshore.
They belonged to rich businessmen of the 1800s.

The Ringling Brothers' Circus used to spend winters in Baraboo. That site is now the Circus World Museum. It presents old-time circus shows in the summer.

▲ **The Circus World Museum in Baraboo hosts shows and parades.**

▲ **Door County is known for its lighthouses.**

The state capitol in Madison stands on an **isthmus,** or narrow strip of land. On either side are lakes. Near the capitol is the Wisconsin Historical Museum. There you'll learn more about Wisconsin's Indians, fur trappers, loggers, and miners.

Wisconsin Dells is a great place for vacations. There the Wisconsin River winds through a deep valley. The river has carved the rocks into strange shapes. Door County is another popular spot. Lighthouses and fishing villages line its coast.

You can go camping or boating along the shore, or wander along nature trails in the forests.

The twenty-two Apostle Islands are scattered in Lake Superior. They offer a great escape from city life. Visitors explore their forests and sandy beaches. The island's museum is an old fur-trading post.

▲ **Kayaking is another great reason to visit Wisconsin's Apostle Islands.**

▲ A carousel for dolls at House on the Rock

In Spring Green, you'll see the awesome House on the Rock. This fourteen-room house perches on top of a rock. Its Infinity Room sticks far out over the valley. The owner collected all sorts of things! You'll see his dollhouses, tiny circuses, and much more.

Nearby is Taliesin. **Architect** Frank Lloyd Wright's home and school are there. Wright believed buildings should blend in with nature. In Wisconsin, you'll find all the wonders of the outdoors combined with many other exciting attractions. See for yourself. Wisconsin is a great place to visit!

Important Dates

1634 Frenchman Jean Nicolet lands at Green Bay.

1673 Jacques Marquette and Louis Joliet travel through Wisconsin.

1763 Wisconsin passes from France to Britain.

1783 Wisconsin becomes part of the United States.

1832 The Black Hawk War is fought.

1836 Wisconsin becomes a U.S. territory.

1848 Wisconsin becomes the thirtieth U.S. state on May 29.

1854 The Republican Party is created in Ripon.

1872 The Wisconsin Dairymen's Association is founded.

1890 Stephen Babcock, a University of Wisconsin professor, creates the Babcock test for milk, which greatly aids the Wisconsin dairy industry.

1901 Governor Robert La Follette Sr. helps launch the Progressive era in Wisconsin.

1919 E.L. "Curly" Lambeau forms the Green Bay Packers.

1957 Milwaukee Braves win the World Series.

1970 Wisconsin senator Gaylord Nelson organizes the first Earth Day.

1971 Several campuses join to form the University of Wisconsin system.

1976 Shirley Abrahamson is the first woman on the Wisconsin Supreme Court.

1980 Speed skater Eric Heiden wins five gold medals in the Winter Olympic Games.

2001 Governor Tommy Thompson becomes U.S. Secretary of Health and Human Services.

Glossary

ancestors—a person's grandparents, great-grandparents, and so on

architect—a person who designs buildings

blacksmiths—people who make metal objects using fire

cultures—groups of people who share beliefs, customs, and a way of life

dairy—relating to milk cows and milk products

industry—a business or trade

isthmus—a narrow strip of land between bodies of water

pioneers—people who explore or settle in a new land

Did You Know?

★ Not many badgers live in the Badger State. The name came from miners in the 1800s. They spent winters in underground shelters that reminded them of badger burrows.

★ The nation's first kindergarten opened in Watertown in 1856.

★ Bloomer is famous as the jump rope capital of the world.

★ Mount Horeb's Mustard Museum contains more than twenty-three hundred kinds of mustard. It's the world's largest mustard collection.

★ Prairie du Sac holds the State Cow Chip Throwing Contest.

★ Wisconsin's 7,446 streams and rivers would stretch 26,767 miles (43,068 km) end-to-end. This is long enough to circle the globe at the equator.

State capital: Madison

State motto: Forward

State nickname: Badger State

Statehood: May 29, 1848; thirtieth state

Area: 56,145 square miles (145,415 sq km); **rank:** twenty-sixth

Highest point: Timms Hill, 1,952 feet (595 m) above sea level

Lowest point: Along Lake Michigan, 581 feet (177 m) above sea level

Highest recorded temperature: 114°F (46°C) at Wisconsin Dells on July 13, 1936

Lowest recorded temperature: –55°F (–48°C) at Couderay on February 4, 1996

Average January temperature: 14°F (–10°C)

Average July temperature: 70°F (21°C)

Population in 2000: 5,363,675; **rank:** eighteenth

Largest cities in 2000: Milwaukee (596,974), Madison (208,054), Green Bay (102,313), Kenosha (90,352)

Factory products: Machinery, foods, paper products, electrical equipment

Farm products: Milk, beef cattle, corn, hay

Mining products: Crushed stone, sand, gravel

State flag: Wisconsin's state flag shows the state coat of arms on a field of blue. The coat of arms has a sailor and a miner on each side of a shield. The shield has symbols for farming, mining, sailing, and manufacturing. In the center is the U.S. coat of arms. This means that Wisconsin is loyal to the United States. Above the shield is a badger because Wisconsin's nickname is the Badger State. "Wisconsin" appears in white above the coat of arms. The date of statehood, 1848, is below the coat of arms.

State seal: The state seal shows the coat of arms.

State abbreviations: Wis. or Wisc. (traditional); WI (postal)

State Symbols

State bird: Robin

State flower: Wood violet

State tree: Sugar maple

State animal: Badger

State wildlife animal: White-tailed deer

State domesticated animal: Dairy cow

State peace symbol: Mourning dove

State fish: Muskellunge

State dog: American water spaniel

State insect: Honeybee

State mineral: Galena

State rock: Red granite

State fossil: Trilobite

State grain: Corn

State soil: Antigo silt loam

State beverage: Milk

State dance: Polka

Making Cranberry Muffins

The 1998–1999 fourth-grade class at Washington School in Merrill suggested the cranberry muffin as the state muffin. This is their recipe.

Makes 15 muffins.

INGREDIENTS:

2 cups flour

1 cup sugar

1 1/2 teaspoons baking powder

1/2 teaspoon baking soda

1 teaspoon salt

1/4 cup butter or margarine

1 egg, beaten

1 teaspoon grated orange peel

3/4 cup orange juice

1 1/2 cups chopped cranberries

DIRECTIONS:

Make sure an adult helps with the hot oven. Preheat oven to 350°F. Sift flour, sugar, baking powder, baking soda, and salt in a large bowl. Cut in the butter until the mixture is crumbly. Stir in the egg, orange peel, and orange juice. Fold in the cranberries. Spoon into muffin cups, filling two-thirds full. Bake 25 to 30 minutes or until golden brown.

"On, Wisconsin!"

Words by Charles D. Rosa and J. S. Hubbard, music by William T. Purdy

On, Wisconsin! On, Wisconsin!
Grand old badger state!
We, thy loyal sons and daughters,
Hail thee, good and great.
On, Wisconsin! On, Wisconsin!
Champion of the right,
"Forward," our motto—
God will give thee might!

Don Ameche (1908–1993) was an actor. His movies include *Trading Places* (1983) and *Cocoon* (1985).

Chris Farley (1964–1997) was a comedy actor. He first appeared on TV's "Saturday Night Live."

Harry Houdini (1874–1926) was a magician known for escaping from tight situations.

Liberace (1919–1987) was a pianist known for his glittery style. His full name was Wladziu Valentino Liberace.

Jackie Mason (1931–) is a comedian.

Georgia O'Keeffe (1887–1986) was an artist who painted huge, colorful flowers and other objects.

William Rehnquist (1924–) was an associate justice (1972–1986) and serves as chief justice (1986–) of the U.S. Supreme Court. Rehnquist was born in Milwaukee.

Spencer Tracy (1900–1967) was a movie actor. Tracy (pictured above left) won two Academy Awards.

Orson Welles (1915–1985) was an actor and motion-picture director. *Citizen Kane* (1941) is his most famous movie.

Gene Wilder (1935–) is an actor. *Young Frankenstein* (1974) is one of his movies.

Laura Ingalls Wilder (1867–1957) wrote the Little House books about pioneer life. *Little House in the Big Woods* (1932) takes place in Wisconsin.

Thornton Wilder (1897–1975) was a playwright and a novelist. He won three Pulitzer Prizes.

Frank Lloyd Wright (1867–1959) was an architect. He designed many famous buildings in his Prairie style.

At the Library

Burns, Diane L., and Cheryl Walsh Bellville (photographer). *Cranberries: Fruit of the Bogs*. Minneapolis: Carolrhoda Books, 1994.

Butler, Dori Hillestad, and Alison Relvea (illustrator). *ABC's of Wisconsin*. Black Earth, Wis.: Trails Media Group, 2000.

Joseph, Paul. *Wisconsin*. Edina, Minn.: Abdo & Daughters, 1998.

Ling, Bettina. *Wisconsin*. Danbury, Conn.: Children's Press, 2002.

Lorbiecki, Marybeth, and Kerry Maguire (illustrator). *Of Things Natural, Wild, and Free: A Story about Aldo Leopold*. Minneapolis: Carolrhoda Books, 1993.

Peterson, Cris. *Century Farm: One Hundred Years on a Family Farm*. Honesdale, Pa.: Boyds Mills Press, 1999.

Zeinert, Karen. *Wisconsin*. Tarrytown, N.Y.: Benchmark Books, 1997.

On the Web

For more information on *Wisconsin,* use FactHound to track down Web sites related to this book.

1. Go to *www.facthound.com*
2. Type in a search word related to this book or this book ID: 0756503280
3. Click on the *Fetch It* button.

Your trusty FactHound will fetch the best Web sites for you!

Through the Mail

Office of the Governor
115 East State Capitol
Madison, WI 53702
For information on Wisconsin's economy

Wisconsin Department of Tourism
201 West Washington Avenue
P.O. Box 7976
Madison, WI 53707
For information on travel and interesting sights in Wisconsin

On the Road

Wisconsin Historical Museum
30 North Carroll Street
Madison, WI 53703
608/264-6555
To learn more about the history of Wisconsin

Wisconsin State Capitol
Capitol Square
Madison, WI 53702
608/266-0382
To visit the state capitol

Index

About the Author

Ann Heinrichs grew up in Fort Smith, Arkansas, and lives in Chicago. She is the author of more than eighty books for children and young adults on Asian, African, and U.S. history and culture. Ann has also written numerous newspaper, magazine, and encyclopedia articles. She is an award-winning martial artist, specializing in t'ai chi empty-hand and sword forms.

Ann has traveled widely throughout the United States, Africa, Asia, and the Middle East. In exploring each state for this series, she rediscovered the people, history, and resources that make this a great land, as well as the concerns we share with people around the world.